Working with young adults

NIACE lifelines in adult learning

The *NIACE lifelines in adult learning* series provides straightforward background and information, accessible know-how and useful examples of good practice for all practitioners involved in adult and community learning. Focusing in turn on different areas of adult learning these guides are an essential part of every practitioner's toolkit.

1. **Community education and neighbourhood renewal** – Jane Thompson, ISBN 1 86201 139 7
2. **Spreading the word: reaching out to new learners** – Veronica McGivney, ISBN 1 86201 140 0
3. **Managing community projects for change** – Jan Eldred, ISBN 1 86201 141 9
4. **Engaging black learners in adult and community education** – Lenford White, ISBN 1 86201 142 7
5. **Consulting adults** – Chris Jude, ISBN 1 86201 194 4
6. **Working with young adults** – Carol Jackson, ISBN 1 86201 150 8
7. **Promoting learning** – Kate Malone, ISBN 1 86201 151 6
8. **Evaluating community projects** – Jane Field, ISBN 1 86201 152 4
9. **Working in partnership** – Lyn Tett, ISBN 1 86201 162 1

Forthcoming titles
10. **Working with Asian heritage communities** – David McNulty, ISBN 1 86201 174 5
11. **Learning and community arts** – Jane Thompson, ISBN 1 86201 181 8
12. **Museums and community learning** – Garrick Fincham, ISBN 1 86201 182 6
13. **Libraries and community learning** – John Pateman, ISBN 1 86201 183 4

The Young Adult Learners Partnership (YALP) is a joint initiative of NIACE and the National Youth Agency. It researches and develops effective approaches to learning and personal development among young adults on the margins of education, training and employment, with the purpose of fostering their capability and their integration as young workers, parents and citizens. The partnership looks at contributory factors affecting individuals' disengagement in learning and design constructive responses that include taking a holistic approach in responding to the needs, interests and aspirations of each young person within motivating learning programmes.

The partnership would like to acknowledge the projects who feature as case studies throughout the publication, and Bryan Merton, Rosemary Napper, Angela Mulverhill and Carolyn Oldfield for their written contributions.

For further information on the work of the partnership please contact Carol Jackson on 0116 285 3736, or Nicola Aylward on 0116 285 3738 or 0116 204 4258.

Websites: www.nya.org.uk and www.niace.org.uk

niace · lifelines in adult learning

6

Working with young adults

Carol Jackson

Published by the National Institute of
Adult Continuing Education (England and Wales)

21 De Montfort Street
Leicester LE1 7GE
Company registration no. 2603322
Charity registration no. 1002775

First published 2003

The *NIACE lifelines in adult learning series* is supported by the Adult
and Community Learning Fund. ACLF is funded by the Department
for Education and Skills and managed in partnership by NIACE and
the Basic Skills Agency to develop widening participation in adult learning.

promoting adult learning

NIACE has a broad remit to promote lifelong learning
opportunities for adults. NIACE works to develop
increased participation in education and training,
particularly for those who do not have easy access
because of barriers of class, gender, age, race,
language and culture, learning difficulties and
disabilities, or insufficient financial resources.

www.niace.org.uk

Cataloguing in Publication Data
A CIP record of this title is available from the British Library

All photographs © Patrick Shéandell O'Carroll, unless otherwise stated
Designed and typeset by Boldface
Printed in Great Britain by Russell Press, Nottingham

ISBN 1 86201 150 8

Contents

Note to the reader
Inspirations: refer to case studies and examples of good practice.
Glossary: the meanings of the words underlined in the text can be found in the glossary on page 40.

1 Policy context and challenge

"In a world where governments no longer exercise much sovereignty either over their defences or over their economies, the best service they can perform for their citizens is to help them be stronger, more responsible, more capable of making decisions and understanding the worlds in which they live. Narrowly this means providing them with skills to make them employable; the habits of being disciplined and flexible, creative and adaptive... More broadly it means helping them to look after themselves and to care for others, helping with life skills and emotional intelligence rather than just the analytical intelligence that older educational systems valued so highly."
Geoff Mulgan, *Life After Politics*, 1997

One of the key policy challenges is how to increase demand for learning particularly among those young adults who are least inclined or able to engage. Recent research carried out by NIACE on adults aged 17 and over indicates that while overall levels of learning among the general population are increasing, the 'learning divide' is still very much in evidence. Opportunities to learn remain heavily weighted in favour of the educationally privileged – those already in employment and education or who have reached a certain threshold of learning.

Since 1997, a series of policy initiatives have been introduced to keep young adults at risk of exclusion in or at least close to learning. These include New Start, New Deal, Learning Gateway and Connexions. Learning mentors and personal advisers have been recruited to remove the barriers to learning and give young adults the intensive support they need to succeed. The Green Paper 14-19: *Extending Opportunities, Raising Standards* (Feb 2002) seeks to make the curriculum more flexible and remove the division between vocational and academic learning which has for generations characterised the landscape in the secondary and tertiary phases of education. It also recognises and gives more value to wider activities such as Citizenship and community based learning initiatives.

But reforms to formal education can only go so far, as they tend to benefit only those who attend. Some of these are reluctant to be in school or college and pose serious challenges to teachers and other learners. Too many young adults have turned their backs on learning and, despite the best efforts of the state, slip through the net.

The key propositions that shape ideas in developing different opportunities for young adults are:

- Socially excluded young adults do not have to be poor to be excluded but they probably are. Although they share many common characteristics, each one is unique and each individual should be regarded differently.
- Young adults are excluded for a number of reasons. There is no single or simple cause. Single agency solutions do not work.
- Some young adults are excluded because of peer pressure. Other young adults are excluded by their peers.
- If young adults are simultaneously given mixed messages about having a wider range of choices and being subject to new constraints, they are bound to be confused. This can compound and complicate their sense of exclusion.

2 Why provide learning opportunities

Motivating disillusioned and underachieving young adults back into learning is a major challenge. But, it is worth doing because many young adults are caught in a tangled web of social problems and they need a range of different opportunities to help them overcome obstacles to learning and in addressing personal problems and social barriers. Providing a range of quality programmes, devised to be attractive to the learner, which hold their interest and stimulate them to achieve and progress is vital if we are to support their development and transition to adulthood and responsible citizenship.

This engagement in worthwhile activity may well improve the quality of their relationships with their friends, family and within the wider community. But they also need to achieve a reasonable degree of emotional stability and a baseline of self-esteem in order to become effective learners and to take advantage of any of the initiatives now open to them as a result of recent Government policy such as the emerging Connexions service.

For government programmes to succeed they have to extend beyond the narrow educational objectives of formal learning and vocational training. They aim to meet broader educational and social purposes and provide all young adults with opportunities to develop fully. They should be viewed by young adults as less of a burden and more of an entitlement. They need to be modern and forward looking, providing a range of opportunities that take account of young adults' individual futures and the kind of world they want to live in. This is particularly true of young adults who have experienced multiple disadvantage.

3 Why a youth work approach works

Many young adults find that they are more able to learn in more informal ways, for example through a youth work approach. A youth work approach is often identified by young adults as being radically different from mainstream provision in its approach, delivery style, structure, methods of assessment and verification and involvement and ownership by the learners. The broad goals of youth work include:

- helping young adults to explore the issues that affect them, make responsible choices;
- encouraging social interaction and compassion;
- promoting self acceptance through positive feedback.

Youth work has long seen itself as encouraging the personal development of young people during their transition to adulthood. It has a special role to play in providing new and different – usually informal – learning opportunities with an emphasis on processes, which encourage personal and social development. Furthermore it has a focus on wider social issues such as the skills and knowledge needed for long-term health and employment.

This approach has a number of defining characteristics:

- it focuses on the interests of the learner and their motivation to learn;
- the learning takes place in accessible environments in which the learners feel comfortable, safe and competent to learn;
- learning is matched to the individuals preferred style and support requirements with the learner at the centre;
- the learners can learn flexibly at a time and pace that most suit them;
- there is ownership of the learning. it is set at their level, negotiated and under-taken in a participatory and empowering way;
- it focuses on the process of learning and the development of personal skills and attributes, rather than academic qualifications;
- incidental learning *en route* is considered as important as the intended learning gain or goals.

It provides a link between:

- the young adults' experiences of exclusion compared to mainstream society;
- the past, present and future;
- youth and adult roles and responsibilities;
- feeling, thinking and doing;
- words and actions in relation to themselves and others.

Examples of projects using this approach are featured throughout this Lifeline including some funded through the Neighbourhood Support Fund (managed by the National Youth Agency) and the Adult and Community Learning Fund (managed by NIACE). These projects have found ways to connect up the experiences of the young adults and the aspirations of public policy to raise levels of participation and achievement in young adults.

The Wild Project

The Wild Project works across Cornwall and seeks to improve the mental, physical and emotional wellbeing of young parents and their children through targeted learning and support opportunities. The work focuses on increasing confidence and self-esteem, reducing post-natal illness, improving community involvement and positive parenting. It offers one-to-one support, advocacy and groupwork with disadvantaged young mothers and fathers under 25 who have not achieved academically, and their children under four.

Wild's approach allows young adults, many of whom who have been out of an academic learning environment since their early teens, to set their own agenda of learning needs and interests and build on their strengths and skills. They compile their own portfolios demonstrating success against agreed learning plans. The project uses Youth Achievement Awards to provide accreditation for skills related to participants' lives, such as decorating a child's bedroom or organising a birthday party.

Having completed these challenges, young adults gain confidence to move onto peer education and those more linked to self-development. Over 80 per cent of young parents' who stay with the project for more than five months move on to further and higher education, employment, self-employment or voluntary work.

INSPIRATIONS

Connect 2 (Derby)

Connect 2 is a joint Life Skills training programme run across Derbyshire through a partnership between Derbyshire Careers and Derby City and Derbyshire youth services. It works with young adults aged 16 to 17 on the Learning Gateway who are identified as needing additional support. Training takes place at six community-based locations throughout the county. Each participant is offered a tailor-made package intended to improve their confidence and motivation, and to help them identify a career aim and progress into employment with training, work-based learning, or further education. Learners attend for at least 16 hours per week for up to 19 weeks, and the programme uses a mix of group activities, skills training, work experience, and a residential event to help them understand the world of work, build confidence, and develop life-skills, self-knowledge and interpersonal skills. It provides the learners with an opportunity to sample different work and learning opportunities. The skills training leads to a range of qualifications including first aid, basic food hygiene, computer literacy and information technology, wordpower and numberpower.

The project has a high success rate relating to attendance and successful transfer into training, work and education. In 2000-01 the retention rate was 89 per cent, with 65 per cent of participants achieving the targets on their individual development plans

4 Providing effective programmes

There are a number of ways of providing learning opportunities and a range of interventions that work for different individuals. Give some thought to what will be most relevant and appropriate for the young adults in the context in which you are working. Here we concentrate on *project working*, which may involve providing support on an individual basis or with a group. It is a valuable and essential part of meeting the needs of young adults because it:

- offers **opportunities to test out and develop new ideas** for the learners and staff;
- allows for **experimentation and taking risks** and a flexible response;
- can **target resources specifically** to particular geographical areas or specific groups of learners;
- can operate with **groups or individuals** or both;
- enables **local ownership** and active involvement of the learners;
- allows **responses to new or different situations**, such as an emerging community issue or to develop a specialist form of provision eg; addressing inequalities or gaps in existing provision;
- can establish the **basis on which other funding can be built** or sought by demonstrating what works.

To 'project' literally means to look forward. Projects can be the focus of change of either people or situations. Projects can take forward ideas, creativity and inspiration and enable them to become a reality. Why do we do projects?

Many reluctant learners who underachieve are not yet ready to achieve the kind of 'hard' academic and vocational outcomes customarily required by funding bodies. Instead they need programmes that are more sensitive to the social characteristics that shape their lives. These programmes should contain learning outcomes that will equip them to become more skilled at interpersonal relations, better self-starters, team workers, problem solvers and independent learners – the qualities often sought by employers.

Fulfilling these outcomes may be undertaken in various ways through:

- **targeted learning and development activities** which are focused on a particular geographical areas, a specific target age group e.g. 16-18 or 16-25 or on a particular theme such as basic skills, young parents etc;

- **activities which are designed to change provision,** practices and people by meeting an identified need or gap and enhancing existing provision such as the provision of one-to-one support mentoring projects;
- **opportunities to try or test out new approaches,** for example, through a particular activity which will interest the learners such as music, outdoor education or motor vehicle/ skateboarding projects or through a residential focus.

The characteristics projects are likely to have in common include:

- delivery over a specified or limited period of time;
- being designed in response to a needs analysis;
- being planned to achieve particular aims and objectives;
- being focused on specified outcomes – the process playing an important part – and valuing unplanned or additional outcomes;
- outcomes and/or learning gain is recorded for the participants;
- being resourced in different ways all targeted to achieve aims objectives and outcomes and to provide the required support;
- the requirement to prepare budgets, keep accounts and produce reports;
- strategies to monitor, review and evaluate the opportunities and activities in order to develop the project;
- celebrating the success of individual learners;
- dissemination of the outcomes of the overall project and for the young adults;
- a range of mechanisms that provide quality assurance;
- equality of opportunity in relation to publicity and recruitment and learning resources used.

Back to basics
Programmes should be based on **four key premises**:

- recognition that young adults are unique individuals with different needs, interests, abilities and aspirations;
- allocation to the young adult learners of a mentor with whom they decide the nature of the project or activity and the combination of outcomes they seek to achieve through it;
- dedication of time to pay attention to the progress and achievement of each individual;
- replacement of a downward spiral of educational failure with a virtuous circle of learning and achievement.

INSPIRATIONS

REMIT 'First Contact' Programme – Leicester

REMIT describes itself as a 'Community Education Mental Health Project.' It was established in 1991 in response to an identified need for a community-based form of learning provision for adults with mental health problems in Leicester. 'First Contact' is a programme specifically aimed at young adults aged 16-30. The objectives of the programme are:

- to provide a safe environment in which people under the age of 30 feel relaxed and empowered;
- to form a bonded self-sufficient group;
- to increase socialisation;
- to increase feelings of confidence among members;
- to challenge negative self-perceptions in members;
- to model healthy social interaction;
- for the group to be self-sufficient within two years.

Described as 'a making friends group,' 'First Contact' runs for two hours per week, for 44 weeks. The structure and content of the programme is initially very informal, often based around simple activities such as games and constructing crossword puzzles. However, through these simple activities, young adults develop the confidence and skills to interact effectively with other members of the group, which can give them the confidence to progress to other courses, which may be accredited.

For many of the young adults referred to REMIT, the key barrier in enabling them to develop independent lives is a lack of confidence and ability to interact with other people. Both practitioners and young adults have testified to the effectiveness of such flexible and learner-centred approaches to meeting the needs of young adults that experience mental health difficulties:

"Young adults with mental health problems can benefit immensely from an educational programme. Initially this could be the reason for getting out of bed in the morning. Setting up a routine, building confidence and making new friends gives a purpose in life, thus helping states of mind and gradually leading to new achievement." (Practitioner)

"Yes, I get the chance to get out and I take my baby out more. I'm mixing with all kinds of people. The benefits are for everything, for my kids, for a job. I don't want to be a burden on anyone." (Young person)

"I've been more positive. I've started thinking about other things to do, going out more. And I speak to people more and ask more questions."

Confidence

Recognition

Motivation

Achievement

It is important that mentors are:

- older and wiser than the young adult;
- inventive in working with the learner and in setting up activities through which; achievements can be demonstrated;
- observant in recording these achievements;
- sensitive in assessing them.

The use of a mentor as guide and assessor adds considerably to the value of the learning experience. The mentor identifies and exploits activities which stimulate the learner and designs a programme in such a way that certain learning outcomes are planned for, at key stages in the process. The young adults are given opportunities to come up with evidence of their achievements through an exercise or a project of their own choice

INSPIRATIONS

Steps Forward Mentoring Programme (Newcastle upon Tyne)

Steps Forward offers basic and social skills education for young adults aged 16-25 who are marginalised by poor educational achievement and social development. It is a partnership between Newcastle Upon Tyne YMCA (host agency), the Newcastle Literacy Trust, the Depaul Trust and the Adult Basic Education Service. Through amalgamating skills from two different professions – youth work and basic skills work – it has developed a new model of practice to reach young adults who were not seeking help from mainstream sources.

Each young person has a trained volunteer mentor who provides one-to-one support to follow an individual learning programme. The project worker and young adults agree individual programmes based on young adultss perceptions of their needs. Young people assess their own progress, and agree an exit strategy based on their personal goals. Both mentors and young adults are offered regular (6 weekly) supervision. The project has provided a mechanism for marginalised young adults to contribute to developing the borough's basic skills strategy, and to feed into the development of Connexions.

Forward Move is part of this project and offers basic skills and social education for young adults aged 16-18 who are involved with the Newcastle Youth Offending Team. It is a partnership between Newcastle YMCA, Depaul Trust and Newcastle Y.O.T. The project works in two settings for those young adults who are incarcerated in Cassington Young Offenders Institute. A worker who is from the De Paul Trust is based within that setting offering support to the young adults and to the mentors. The second aspect of the work is the community element, to ensure continuity of practice allowing the young adults to keep the same mentor. This worker is based within the Newcastle YMCA Steps Forward and works to the ethos of that project.

INSPIRATIONS

Befrienders

The Befrienders project in Barking and Dagenham uses learning mentors to provide advice, support and guidance to young people who have difficulties within formal education. Before a young person joins the project they are matched with a mentor who 'befriends' them. Once they are ready the young person will then progress onto the Getting Connected programme with the support and guidance of their mentor. A recent success was a young joiner who with her mentor's help wrote to the Head of Lifelong Learning explaining her circumstances and requesting a place on a college course which was full. He was so impressed, the course suddenly grew a vacancy!

All Change

This arts charity uses DJ and other media skills to inspire young adults into learning. The organisation currently runs two youth work projects – 2Stepz and Drop in the Mix – which tackle social exclusion through music programmes offering DJ mixing, keyboard tuition, CD burning and lyric writing. Outreach workers meet young adults around estates who may be disruptive to other residents and attract them to mobile and centre-based provision. Support workers ensure that programmes take account of needs and interests of individual young adults, offer advice and support, and help young adults record their progress. The project works closely with other local providers such as careers, lifelong learning centres, youth work teams, lifeskills providers and Connexions to provide young adults with access to alternative pathways to learning.

5 Exploring 21st century skills

In youth work a variety of vehicles are used to encourage the acquisition of particular skills and levels of understanding relating to the broad areas outlined above. It is usually through these activities that the development of what are referred to as 'soft skills' takes place. The easy way of defining soft skills is to think of what is needed for everyday living in the 21st century. These include working with others, problem solving and negotiation skills. They also include personal qualities such as increased self-confidence and esteem, motivation, acknowledging and managing feelings and being self aware, with the determination and a willingness to learn.

It is vital that more ways are found to recognise, value and reward the skills and qualities that young adults develop as a result of their involvement in these projects. *Getting Connected* – a curriculum framework for social inclusion is designed to promote and develop such skills especially those concerned with young adults' emotional literacy.

Getting Connected – a curriculum framework for social inclusion

This framework aims to give young adults recognition for achieving 'soft skills'. Increasingly, young adults are demanding that their achievements have currency, so this curriculum includes the option of assessment and accreditation through the **Profile of Personal Development** awarded by one of the premier national awarding bodies, the OCR (Oxford, Cambridge and RSA). The skills are identified and recorded in a portfolio and if desired can be submitted for accreditation.

The curriculum framework is distinctive in its:

- **content:** it concentrates as much on feelings, attitudes and behaviour – the domain of emotional literacy – as on skills, knowledge and understanding.
- **nature:** it specifies learning outcomes and gives much sharper definition to the goals of personal development which have always tended to be expressed in vague terms. These outcomes can be mapped against those specified in key and basic skills, offering scope for dual accreditation.
- **flexibility:**
  - the selection of outcomes and the means of achieving them are determined by the young adult learners themselves in consultation with a mentor;
  - different forms of assessment can be used including self and peer assessment;

    – progress towards the outcomes can be recorded through a portfolio which can be submitted to OCR for accreditation

- **method:** young adults can map their own progress through projects and activities in which they choose to take part. Examples might include music, dance and drama; outdoor pursuits; motor vehicles. These provide the context for achieving the learning outcomes.
- **context:** the framework is particularly well suited to being used in informal settings – such as youth and community projects and on residential experiences.

A curriculum framework for social inclusion

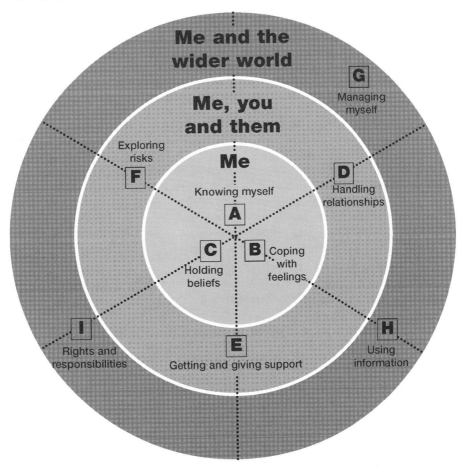

6 Delivering in practice

The value of a partnership approach

Because so many of the challenges facing disadvantaged young adults are complex and inter-connected, providers of learning and skills are encouraged to work in partnership with other agencies to ensure that a more holistic or integrated approach is taken. This is more likely to enable young adults to be seen as individuals.

Partnership or interagency working is not easy and takes time but the benefits outweigh the costs. The principal benefit is the enhancement of programmes, projects and practice arising from the range of approaches and styles used by the individuals through sharing experiences, perspectives, skills, knowledge, workload and administrative procedures.

For inter-agency work to be effective it is helpful to have some agreement between partners based on some of the following guidelines:

- ensure sufficient time for the planning and development of the programme allowing for joint ownership;
- be clear about line management of the project on a day-to-day basis and ensure that communication is established between all organisations involved. this is especially important if there is a steering group or support group;
- agree communication strategies such as reporting responsibilities and dissemination strategies;
- enable synergy between practitioners through joint training; this may focus on the principles underlying the programme, planning sessions, negotiating ground rules, agreeing monitoring, review and evaluation procedures;
- ensure that a process for recording evidence of learning and achievement is in place at all stages of the programme and this is understood and valued by all involved. this is especially important for the learners in that they will have something to evidence their achievements when they progress onto other learning opportunities;
- clarify responsibilities, detailing which agency or organisation is responsible for, among other things:
  - recording attendance and participation
  - identifying needs
  - providing resources and materials

- oversight of any internal assessment process
- arrangements for quality review of the programme including how resources are allocated, how learning is assessed and evidence of achievement is collected.

INSPIRATIONS

Neighbourhood Support Funds

Three Neighbourhood Support Fund projects in Hackney are working in partnership to offer support to young adults who are not attending college as well as improving relations in the local community. Education for Choice, Immediate Theatre and Clapton Community Housing Trust have set up a group called STRATEGY which gives young adults the chance to meet, share and relax in an informal atmosphere. The groupwork culminated in a live performance, involving drama, rap, singing, mixing and short films made by the young adults.

Step Project (Gloucestershire)

This multi-agency initiative led by Gloucestershire Youth and Community Service and Cirencester College targets socially excluded young adults aged 16-25 in what is generally an affluent rural area. It provides confidence building, individual learning needs assessment, basic skills support, IT skills development and access to vocational training. By April 2002 the project had supported over 100 young adults, including specific provision for young mothers.

The project was initially funded through SRB, but since April 2002 has been embedded in the Connexions Service. Through the college it has a contract for Learning Gateway lifeskills provision. Each young person works with a project worker (employed by Cirencester College but based in the youth centre) to identify their needs and draw up an action plan. These include personal, lifeskills and other targets which are measurable and therefore recordable, linking into national qualifications wherever possible. Where appropriate young adults are teamed up with volunteer mentors who provide further informal support. Many young adults are referred on and supported to start vocational training or employment. Eighty per cent of young adults who make more than a single contact with the project have progressed either into employment or into further training.

INSPIRATIONS

Route 43 Mentoring Plus – Manchester (NSF)

This mentoring project receives funding from the Neighbourhood Support Fund (NSF) for disaffected young adults aged 15-19 in South Manchester, overseen by a multi-agency steering group with representation from the youth service, youth offending team, Manchester College of Technology, the chief executive's department and other organisations. Using the 'mentoring plus' model developed by Dalston Youth Project (Crime Concern), it offers participants one-to-one support from a volunteer mentor, plus a year-long programme of activities, support and accredited learning opportunities (for instance, word and number power, first aid and sports leadership). Young people develop individual action plans with staff, and assess their own progress against these. The range of activities includes groupwork sessions in numeracy, literacy and lifeskills, ICT, taster courses in areas such as music, sport, first aid and work experience, and advice and information. It also offers trips out, residential events, and college programmes. The project encourages young adults to develop responsibility for running the activities. They are represented on both the steering group and the advisory group, and assist in the recruitment and training of mentors and staff.

Project design and work plans

Projects are shaped around the available resources whether through external funding from a range of different sources or from a mainstream budget. The details need to be worked out before the delivery of the programme can take place. The aims, objectives and outcomes agreed in addition to the funding sources become the controls for the design of the project. If external funding has been secured it is likely that the key activities, partners, aims, objectives, outcomes and any milestones for the project will have been determined. This Is also true for internally funded initiatives. It is vital at this stage to establish what is feasible to achieve as the ideas and the actual implementation may be very different for a variety of reasons. Using the SMART system is a good way of drawing up the project design and work plan.

S = Specific   Is it really clear what the project is intending to achieve? Is it broken down into small steps and is it easily understood?

M = Measurable How will you know what the project or an individual learner has achieved?

A = Achievable What resources are needed to achieve the outcomes? Are all the things in place that are needed to implement the project?

R = Relevant   Does the project meet a defined need – how might it become more relevant? Do the learning outcomes have the same relevance?

T = Time scale   When will the outcomes be achieved – is there sufficient time to ensure they are met? At what points will celebration take place when the outcomes have been met? Is there sufficient time built in to review them?

It is important that all those involved in the project have an opportunity to determine whether the targets and outcomes are SMART, as this is an excellent way of testing out if the ideas can be implemented and if they will meet the intended outcomes.

It is important that where external funding is involved that communication is kept open with the funding body. There may be particular guidelines, which are not only very useful but will need to form part of the project design. This might include when the funding can be drawn down, when reports and accounts must be submitted, what exactly the funding will pay for and what monitoring and evaluation is expected.

Producing a work plan can help in creating a structure for the project as it sets out the timetables for the activities to be planned, delivered, reviewed and reported on. It also provides an opportunity for all involved to share the practicalities of implementation. Any partner organisations will also need to be involved in this process.

The work plan

An opportunity needs to be found at the beginning of any new project for all those involved with the project to discuss the work plan and agree how it will be written and by whom? The plan should be shared with the team before it is finalised. Start with the aims and objectives of the project:

- what activities will need to be undertaken and when?
- who will carry them out?
- what are the required resources?

Think about the time-scale of the project, the sequence of activities and the costs of each stage. It is important to consider whether the people involved have the skills, knowledge, support and time to successfully complete the activities. Staff training and development may need to be included in the plan as well as a planning and starting phase. Marketing and promotion of the project will need to be included in the plan in addition to the day-to-day activities, review meetings, partnership meetings, monitoring stages, evaluation and dissemination activities, reporting and accounting dates and celebrating achievement.

Programme of activity

This is determined by a number of factors, which need consideration.

Resources available

Those that might support the learners, for example, travel costs, childcare, support and refreshments. The staff and volunteer time available to develop the project including the amount of support time required. The resources from any partners organisations will need to be clarified.

Needs of the learners

It is important that these are identified at the outset and continually reviewed to ensure the project and activities are meeting the changing needs. The young adult learners will gain more from any learning opportunity if they have the chance to negotiate the pace at which they learn, how they best learn, what will help them and if they are supported at different stages of the process.

Individual or group work

In devising programmes and projects for young adult learners which are designed to enhance their self-esteem, confidence and skills it is important at the outset to decide whether to:

- use a group work approach – with substantial support for individual learners;
- base the learning entirely on a one-to-one mentoring approach;
- combine the two approaches – this might depend on the resources available, particularly the paid staff and volunteers.

Some learners will find it easier to start on a one-to-one basis. If this is the case, then the following questions have to be considered:

- Is there the commitment of time and the provision of systems within the organisation to support the individual?

- Can the individual access learning through group work at a later stage if that is chosen?
- Can the one-to-one approach be used to supplement the group work approach?

If a group work approach is taken then the following questions have to be considered:

- Are the resources available – minimum group size, reasonable staff/learner ratio, safe accessible and comfortable venue, reliable and affordable transport, facilities and resources to support the learners needs, such as access to a crèche?
- Is the group going to follow a common theme or activity?
- How long will the project or activity last?
- Is recruitment going to be at a fixed point or will there be a roll-on and roll-off recruitment, with allowances made to incorporate new learners into an existing group?
- How is support for individual learners to be provided for within the group?
- What use can be made of a peer tutoring or 'buddy' system for joiners of the group?
- How is evidence of individuals' learning to be secured within a group project?
- Do staff have sufficient understanding and skills in group processes?

Whichever approach or combination is adopted it is important that there is continuing review and evaluation of the process by the learners and the staff. Evaluative meetings are useful in highlighting any changes that might be helpful or to advise on learning styles being selected.

Delivering the project

Once the programme of activity has been decided upon and the partnerships and work-plans have been agreed, the actual project can begin. The stages of implementation can be recorded on the work-plan and individuals can create their own development or action plans to record the achievement of developmental goals towards an overall project aim. Individuals such as the project co-ordinator, the youth workers, the guidance workers and support mentors can have their individual action plans to evidence how they have worked towards achieving the goals of the project.

Keeping recordings

It is vital that in any work with young adults, recordings are kept to benefit the learners themselves as a way of evidencing their achievement or learning gain. The recordings can be a combination of their own recordings and observations and those of the project workers. Accurate recordings of particular milestones and outcomes are very useful as a way of demonstrating the outcomes and success of the project, and particularly useful in continuing to secure future funding.

It is important that there are opportunities to identify and record the acquisition and development of the skills and attributes of young adult learners and for someone else to verify them.

Keeping things going

Be clear whether the nature of the work and the contact with the learners in the project is short, medium or long term, as this will highlight different aspects of sustainability. In general, the sustainability of projects depends on the following aspects, which need to be built in at the outset.

- **Resources**
  Funding is vital to get things going. In the long run, it is better to seek funding from a variety of sources and link the project to local issues, concerns and needs rather than dream up a new project to fit with funding criteria.
- **Knowledge**
  Opportunities need to be built in for the learners to acquire new or relevant knowledge to meet their needs and aspirations.
- **Skills**
  It is important to recognise and make the most of the skills that young adults already have as well as creating opportunities to teach new skills and handing over the responsibilities that go with applying them.

INSPIRATIONS

Care2Share
(Brighton and Hove)

This is a youth centre-based peer education programme matching young adults aged 16 to 25 who have become disengaged from formal education with tutors within the same age range. The learners undergo an initial learning needs assessment with the C2S development worker, and are then matched with one or more peer tutors, who undertake training to prepare them for this role. Tutors then support learners in working towards agreed learning goals, which are demonstrated through portfolios created using a variety of methods including web-pages and CD-ROM. The development worker monitors the progress of both learners and tutors. As an integral part of the project, tutors and learners run a snack bar at the youth centre. This ensures that they acquire a range of skills at a practical level, such as project management, budgetary and money-handling skills, shopping, customer service and catering skills. Young people have a strong role in shaping the project's design and delivery, and hold regular team meetings to assess its development. Young people have the opportunity to have their achievement recognised in various ways; in 2002-03 the project aims to support half of its learners to achieve formal accreditation.

7 Why is learning important in supporting young adults?

Learning is an essential life skill. To move forward with our lives, it's vital that we learn from the experiences that come our way. We need to:

- avoid repeating mistakes (although some people argue there are no mistakes, only 'unintended consequences' or 'opportunities for learning'!);
- build on what we are good at;
- try to fill in the gaps in our skills, knowledge and understanding where they seem to be holding us back;
- change those things we are unhappy with.

Learning is a lifelong activity – we need to learn, continually, to develop and adapt to the changing environment.

Many of us are motivated to do so, because we are committed to our own growth and development as individuals. Also, if learning has been positive for us – it is likely to have added skills and qualifications that give us access to stimulating and rewarding work.

However, for many young adults on the margins, learning 'sucks'. They will probably:

- have had a bad – and sometimes humiliating – experience of education and left school as soon as they were able to;
- be short of some of the basic and key skills;
- lack the motivational and self-management skills (such as organising their time and resources) that are essential for independent learning.

Effective programmes and projects aim to provide positive learning experiences, with a different atmosphere from school. They use activities in which the young adults are already interested as the 'hook' for re-engaging them in learning.

Before going any further, complete the following stages.

1. Write down three examples of things you have learned over the last three months.
2. For each item in the list, answer the following questions:

a) Was it planned or unintended learning?
b) Did any particular events stimulate your learning?
c) Did you use any of the following? If so, note them, and add others:

Friends   Watching a demonstration
Internet   Books and magazines
TV or computer programme   Radio
Manual   Experiment on your own

So *how* did you do learn? If you were to explain how you learned best to someone else, what would you say? Note down your response.

Think about any young adults you are working with – what has prompted or prevented their learning? Note down your response.

Learning from experience

It is commonly said that experience is the best teacher, that we learn best by doing something. Being told what to do, reading about it or watching other people do it can take us some of the way. The best way to remember and learn is to do it, reflect, apply what we learned from the reflection and think about how we will try it again before doing so.

(a) The Learning Cycle (after David Kolb)

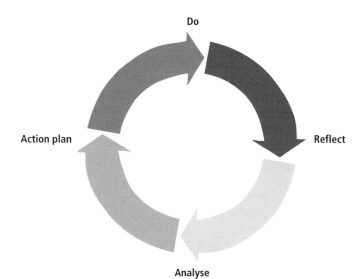

Do

Reflect

Analyse

Action plan

An **Experience** might trigger our desire to learn. It might be a starting point for our learning. However – we don't always learn from experience! (Think of the number of times you have repeated the same mistakes!) We need to use the other parts of the cycle.

Reflection involves reviewing the experience and our responses to it – asking, for example, *'What did I do?' And then what happened?' 'What was I thinking about, at the time?'* And afterwards? *'How did I feel while I was doing it / thinking that? How did I feel afterwards?'* As we reflect on our experiences, we work out their personal significance to us.

When we **Analyse** a situation or experience, we take a step back from it. We try to make sense of the experience – and our responses to it – by looking at it in a broader context. To do this we need to find a theory that allows us to think about the experience in a more abstract way and make generalisations. Sometimes we come up with our own theory, though we'll not necessarily call it that! Sometimes we use those developed by others.

Action planning emphasises our personal capacity to **change**. We don't always have to act the same way. In this phase, we use our **reflection** and **analysis** to decide what to do differently in future. It might be specifically for the next time we find ourselves in the same situation (or want to avoid it). It might involve transferring the know-how to other situations. An important part of action planning is taking steps to make sure we implement our action plan! Action planning involves a fundamental commitment to getting things right for ourselves.

Young adult learners may need some help in going through this cycle. Encourage them to think back on their experience, trace consequences back to causes, and work out for themselves why things happened the way they did.

Activity
Try this yourself.

Step 1
Think of some key learning experiences in your life that led to significant changes in the way you thought about or acted in the world. They might have been short and sudden experiences or longer and slower. For example:

- going to school for the first time;
- having a big row with somebody you care deeply about;
- losing something precious to you;
- finding you could do something other people could but you never thought you would be able to.

Step 2

Take a single sheet of paper and draw horizontal lines along it and divide it into eight equal parts as set out below. Use one sheet for each experience and label it. Then answer the following questions:

What happened?	
What started it?	
What did you learn?	
What words describe how you felt while it was happening?	
Who else was involved?	
Did they help or hinder your learning? How?	
How would you describe the learning process?	
What were the key things that happened during this process as compared with other events when you did not learn as much?	

Step 3

Look back on these sheets and seek out if there were any things that were common in the experiences – in how things happened and what you felt for example. Can you see any patterns here?

Then use the same sheets to list the factors that helped you learn and those that got in the way

Things that helped me learn	Things that hindered me learning

(b) Learning styles

You should now have a good sense of how your key learning experiences may have equipped you with the skills you now have. You should know more about patterns in your learning and what your preferred learning style is. You can match your learning style against the learning cycle mentioned at the start of this. This may be a useful tool to enable young adults to identify their preferred learning style. It may help them understand why their experience of learning has not been particularly positive and what they could change for themselves in the future.

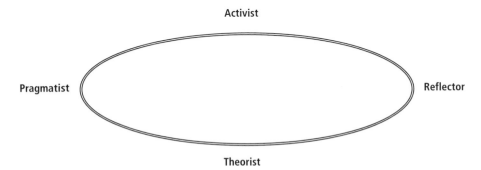

Activists want to get on with it – now! They tend to loathe theories and want plenty of hands-on experiences. They cannot be bothered with instruction manuals, they want to try things out to see how they work. They often enjoy working with others as long as they learn in the same way.

Reflectors like to take time considering, imagining and talking around things, finding out what other people think and how they see things. They like to think about their own responses. After seeing a film they like to think about it before giving their opinion. They enjoy watching how other people behave.

Theorists like an framework in which to understand the world and often create their own. They like to read, speculate, listen to what other people have to say, enjoy ideas and may seem detached from 'the real world'. They enjoy trading ideas and see how they fit together. They look for patterns and use them to explain the world.

Pragmatists tend to be great list makers. They like looking for new ideas and techniques to apply to situations and problems. They tend to plan carefully for what needs to be done. They like to get on with things and know what the goal is, and what resources they can use to help them achieve it.

What do you think you are? Or are you a mixture of each. Or is your preferred learning style affected and influenced by the people you are with or the problem or task at hand?

- Do you have a preferred learning style?
- Do you recognise any of the above traits in people that you know?
- What effect does a preferred learning style have on your taste in learning methods?

Think about it. Think how, if you have preferred learning styles, young adults are likely to as well. How will you find out? What will you do with the information you collect? How will it influence your practice?

Feedback

Giving and receiving feedback is an important part of learning. Having done a project, programme or piece of work we need to know how we have done. Only then can we know how to improve. This is part of assessment, an aspect of learning which makes us apprehensive because it reveals weaknesses as well as strengths. And we do not like to be shown up for coming up short.

The giving of feedback is a skill. It can be done well allowing the person receiving it to deepen their understanding and knowledge about themselves. Or it can be done badly leaving the recipient feeling depressed with no idea how to improve next time.

Ten tips to giving <u>feedback</u> (This can apply to practitioners and young adults):

1. Find out what the person to whom you are giving feedback thinks about how they have done.
2. Make clear that you are offering feedback as one equal to another.
3. Make sure you do not tell the person what to do; instead encourage them to make their own decision about how to do better next time; if they ask for advice, by all means give it.
4. Be genuine with your praise; if you are being insincere it will be picked up.
5. Reinforce the positives; when receiving feedback most people tend to concentrate on the negatives; so begin and end with positive points (see note about feedback sandwich below).
6. If you are critical, try and be constructive by suggesting ideas about how things could be done differently.
7. Criticise the action or what was done, not the person who did it.
8. Keep negative comments short; the more time spent dwelling on something the more likely it is to happen again.
9. Be specific about both the positives and negatives; comments like "you were great" or "that was awful" are not helpful; in what respects did someone do well or not so well?
10. Compare an individual's performance with how they have done before, not with their peers; that makes people anxious and mistrustful.

The feedback sandwich

As with most sandwiches, the most important thing about the feedback sandwich is the **filling**. This is the piece of feedback from which the person receiving it has most to learn, where they can pick up clues on how they might do better next time.

Keep it brief and straightforward but make it memorable so that the flavour lingers on; use the A B C – **Accurate, Brief and Clear**.

Aim for a **balance of tastes**, a balance of positives and negatives but make sure you start and end with a positive comment.

Also the key to a good sandwich is its **freshness**. The sooner the feedback is given after the event or performance the better.

8 Monitoring, reviewing, evaluating and disseminating

It is vital that strategies for monitoring, reviewing and evaluation are established from the beginning of the project and incorporated into the work-plan.

Monitoring

Monitoring is the process of checking that activities, goals and outcomes (for the project and the young adults) are taking place as planned. Reviewing the work-plan on a regular basis ensures the progress is taking place as originally planned. If there are deviations from the plan, these should be noted, assessed and analysed to fully understand the differences. Amendments and additions can then be made, in consultation with line managers, to ensure the work continues to meet the overall goals.

Financial monitoring

Financial monitoring is an important aspect. Budgets need to be drafted in line with organisational or sponsors' guidelines. Responsibility for coding and recording expenditure should be determined at the outset. Monitoring expenditure against the budget should be held regularly and reported as appropriately to the Project Manager under the Management Group. It is helpful if claims and monitoring reports are submitted at the same time and the dates recorded on the plan of work.

Reviewing

Reviewing involves reflection or looking back on activities, events, and phases of development in order to find out what people think and feel. Opportunities to review need to be for everyone and at different stages throughout the project. They can be held on an individual basis or in groups. This includes the learners, the practitioners, providers, partners and management or advisory group.

Reviews provide an opportunity for changing and adapting practice and can be either formative (shaping or forming) or summative (summarising at the end). It is vital for the young adults that regular reviews take place, which help identify their progression routes and supports them to follow this through. When the young adults have moved on from the project, it is crucial to have at least one follow up review to find out about their progress.

Opportunities need to be provided for individual reflection, as this may be the most appropriate for some learners (refer to learning styles). It is, however, important that there are ways to be found to share key thoughts and feelings as they will inform the continuing and future developments of the project and can include notes in a diary, meeting notes, or through an action plan.

Photography, drama, music, creative writing and other art forms may be one way of enabling groups or individuals to express what they have learned or gained as a result of involvement in the project. Information from reviews can feed into the wider process of evaluation.

Evaluating

Evaluating is the process of establishing whether the aims and objectives are being met, and identifying what difference the project has made. Key questions to consider include:

- Is the project achieving what it set out to do, in the way it planned?
- Is it making a difference to the learners, practitioners, providers and partners?
- How is the difference being identified and recorded?
- Is it having an impact on the wider community?
- Are there any unintended consequences, outcomes or benefits (or otherwise) being observed, identified or reported?
- What works best, and why?
- What seems to be less effective, and why?

Information from reviews needs to be regularly collated and presented to the management or partnership group who should ask evaluative questions, along with project staff and managers. Any evaluation needs to inform the ongoing development of the project and be used to make recommendations, which can inform future work.

It is sometimes possible to appoint (dependent on funding) an external evaluator at the beginning of a new project. They can work alongside the different elements of a project including all those involved with it to capture their responses. The evaluation needs to be regarded as one of the most fundamental parts of a project as it is through this process that the effectiveness of a project in achieving its aims can be identified.

Evaluation is the mechanism that can identify what everyone has learned as a result of being involved in the project. It provides the instrument through which recommendations about changes in practice are *identified* and good practice is shared.

Disseminating

Letting people know about the work being undertaken is important for four main reasons:

- It helps spread the word locally, which can encourage more people to be involved;
- It communicates a sense of energy and action and the feeling that something good is going on;
- It helps keep other organisations, partners and funding bodies on board;
- It demonstrates the value of particular activities, approaches and methodologies.

Disseminating outcomes of evaluation can be as imaginative and creative as possible, for example, musical presentations, dance and drama, photographs, exhibitions, and so on, and needs to be available to as wide an audience as possible. In addition to friends and family of the participants, and others living and working in the local community, it is important that the press hear about any good news stories. Briefings and updates are useful to keep local politicians, partners and funding bodies informed, for example, the Connexions service, the Learning Partnerships and the local Learning and Skills Councils.

The dissemination has greater impact if the following can be included:

- testimonies or stories from the participants;
- photographs which illustrate activity;
- examples of the impact of the work and any evidence of the benefits of learning.

This testimony is from one of the participants taking part in the YMCA Neighbourhood Support Fund Project – the Lifeskills course in Leicester.

'I felt I had no one. I had fallen out with my mum and I was living with my boyfriend. I was suffering depression at the time when I went to the hospital school that is why I felt I had no-one helping me. Then I went to a career point and they helped me as they put me on a course at the YMCA. I was really scared when I had to start as I had not been anywhere for about a year but when I started I said to myself that this is it, if you want the help then this is where I have to start. So I did!

What am I like now at Lifeskills ?

I have the confidence to go out with my friends and come out of my house and come to the YMCA. I look forward to coming as I love to get out and this makes me feel like I am doing something with my life again. This was a big step for me and I am glad I made that step.

Everyone at Lifeskills made me feel proud of myself. That is why I have the confidence to be here today , I know that they will help me move on to the next big step in my life, when I feel I am ready to move on. I have already learnt a lot of skills since I have been at the YMCA.

Now I have looked at what I have done, writing this makes me feel proud of myself, what I have done for myself and I have a lot of confidence and know what I want to do with myself and what the next step I need to take is – and that is going to college

9 Celebrating

Celebrating the work of the project can mark achievements of many kinds, including group and individual achievement as well as different stages of the project's development. Any celebration is likely to help raise the profile of the particular project or piece of work. They can also be useful as one way of informing the wider world of successful outcomes. They help to endorse the work of the project staff and provide an opportunity to put the spotlight on the learners or participants; they can be a public recognition of the achievements and provide further encouragement to individuals and groups.

Careful thought needs to be given in drawing up the invitation list. In addition to staff volunteers and participants it may need to include representatives of partner organisations and community groups, the steering or management group, sponsors and statutory services. The families and friends of the participants should be invited, as way of endorsing the significance of the achievement, the learning journey, to support the learners and may even encourage others to take part.

Photo courtesy of YMCA

Photo courtesy of YMCA

There are many ways to celebrate the work of the project, and these can include:

- performances;
- exhibitions or displays;
- award ceremonies;
- days out;
- residential events.

All of which are quite high profile and require a lot of planning and organisation. Publishing newsletters, photographs, letters and creative writing are also effective in celebrating the outcomes of the project and disseminating them to a wider audience – whether for individuals or groups. A participant telling the story of their involvement in the project can be an extremely powerful way of demonstrating the difference it has made to them. Inviting the radio and local press to promote or attend an event will further contribute to this.

10 Letting go and moving on

In recognising the enormous amount of commitment many people have in supporting young adults to learn, it is important that we are responsible and ethical about what we do – the young adult learners do not have a choice about the range of issues they are confronted with. The term exit route or exit strategy is often used in describing procedures put in place for finishing projects, letting go and moving on. It is vital to ensure that at the conclusion of the project the young adult learners are not left without a place to go. It is important that they have an opportunity to reflect on their achievement and gain either verbal or written recognition, as this will continue to build their confidence and motivation and enable them to make a positive progression. Where there has been a mentor relationship with individuals, it is important to 'end' the process giving both parties the opportunity to contribute to a summary discussion and to agree what activity may be done as the conclusion.

If the project is continuing with new learners while the current group move on, it is important that they are aware of support available to them and ways are found to track their progress. This might not be possible for all projects to secure on their own, other partner organisations may have a key role to play in this and it must be clear how this will operate.

If the project is time limited, it is important this is clear from the outset and if changes take place en route affecting it, it is important that people are kept informed.

11 Check it out

Good practice, challenges and trouble shooting

Good practice

- Starts with identifying gaps in provision for young adult learners and establishing how to meet specific identified needs. This needs to be done in a consultative and participating way, focusing on the young adults.
- Relates to the wider social, cultural and economic context in which the young adults are situated as well as to their individual interests, concerns, abilities and aspirations.
- Dedicates time to attend to the progress and achievement of the individual.
- Works to remove barriers to learning and participation and supports young adults by the allocation of a mentor with whom they decide on the outcomes they seek to achieve and receive guidance and support from.
- Agrees its aims and objectives based on the above factors.
- Uses community-based accessible venues where young adults feel comfortable and which are attractive, welcoming and safe, available at a suitable time and has sufficient space and resources.
- Works to replace a downward cycle of educational failure with a virtuous circle of learning and achievement.
- Provides option of accreditation for the learners.
- Has a clear focus on planned outcomes of the project and provides opportunities to identify unintended outcomes.
- Celebrates achievement throughout the life of the project and supports the young adults into further opportunities, according to their individual aims and aspirations.
- Identifies roles and responsibilities of staff involved in the project and engages staff with the appropriate skills, knowledge and experience who are sensitive to the needs of learners, and who adapt an empowering participatory approach.
- Manages staff by offering clear action planning, review and support in relation to workload, the outcomes of the project, and health and safety.
- Encourages constructive partnerships and clarifies roles, expectations and responsibilities.
- Forms management or steering groups to support and assist the development and outcomes of the project.

- Promotes equality of opportunity in all its practices, curriculum materials, and adopts open, clear policies in relation to discrimination by gender, faith, race, sexuality and ability.
- Disseminates the outcomes of the project to wider, interested audiences as a way of sharing good practice and informing future developments.
- Recognises and plans for all stages of the project including its exit, which might include accessing additional funding, securing it as mainstream funded provision or supporting strands of activity with a range of organisations.

Challenges

- Projects can have an element of risk as they try out new and different ways of working, which may be a real challenge to all involved as some partner organisations may feel their reputation rests on the outcomes of the project.
- Projects can be seen as outside the mainstream of the organisation, which can be isolating for the youth workers involved.
- Recruiting, supporting, and developing staff to deliver effective high-quality work with young adults who have not been actively engaged in learning opportunities takes time and energy. It is all the more complicated if the staff contracts are short term due to funding constraints.
- Short-term funding can often mean a requirement that the money needs to be spent quickly and may leave the future of the project somewhat uncertain.
- The establishment and development of a new project takes a significant amount of time, and the intended outcomes for the learners may not occur in the specified time because of external factors, the nature of the relationship with the staff and the individuals needing to work at their own pace.
- The needs and priorities of young adults may change substantially over short periods of time and will impact on the responsiveness and flexibility of the project.
- Finding ways to demonstrate that learning has taken place or that the young adults have developed their skills and qualities can be a challenge itself.

Trouble shooting

- Conducting a risk assessment at the beginning of a new project is one way to identify potential difficulties and highlight contingency plans. A supportive and pragmatic approach will help, especially if the project has a number of different strands, or involves a range of partner organisations. Being clear about roles, responsibilities and agreeing strategies to work together will be important.
- If projects have a positive public relations strategy with the participants, the organisations, the sponsors and the community will help. It is also important to recognise, value, and build on the links within/across a range of organisations and know that it takes time for a new project to demonstrate its value.

- Being as realistic as possible about the nature of the learners, the levels of support they may require, external factors that might help or hinder their progress, and the intended outcomes of the project are extremely important.
- Listening to learners and consulting with them at all stages of the project is a vital part of ensuring the provision continues to meet their needs.
- Identifying and recording any learning, skills or qualities being developed as a result of involvement in the project is vital for the benefit of the learners themselves and the project. It is important to recognise the time this takes and the need for a system of recording this information to be in place at the beginning of the project. Reviews with the young adults needs to be carried out regularly. There are a variety of tools/recording systems that may assist with this.
- Considering different funding sources for the continuation of the project will be important. Being open and honest about the purpose, time-scale and the likely ending of the project will enable the young adults to see the intentions of the project as being genuine.
- Recruitment of project staff needs to match the anticipated roles within the project, the levels of responsibility and the knowledge, skills and experience required. The process needs to take account of the time required between appointment and start date, and staff need to be included in development and training activities which supports their work in the project, and helps create routes for their wider professional and personal development.
- Deploying permanent staff to work in projects, and substituting temporary staff to cover them, can help in alleviating the constraints of short-term funding, finding the match of skills and experience, and providing developmental opportunities for less experienced colleagues.
- It is important to be flexible in creating, developing, and maintaining quality provision for young adults. The changing needs, priorities, and aspirations will need to be taken into account, and their views and involvement in making changes to the provision incorporated. Enough flexibility in staffing levels and resources to deliver the provision within such a changing world is crucial.

Glossary of terms

<u>Barriers to learning</u> – These can relate to aspects of a person's life preventing them from taking part in learning opportunities or their levels of self-esteem. These may include: previous negative experiences of education and learning, lack of transport and childcare in the local area, insufficient resources, not feeling motivated and or not interested.

<u>Connexions</u> – The recently developed service operating in England for young adults aged 13-19 offering the 'best start in life for every young person'. The support for young adults is provided through personal advisers.

<u>Emotional literacy</u> – Refers to a range of 'aptitudes' that people need to develop if they are to function effectively with each other and as learners. A necessary ingredient of emotional literacy is self-esteem. Other key aptitudes include self-awareness, empathy and motivation.

<u>Empathy</u> – Understanding the feelings of others and taking account of them in day-to-day behaviour. An ability to manage ones own feelings knowing when it is appropriate to express feelings and when it is not and how to express both good and bad feelings without unduly upsetting other people.

<u>Exit strategy</u> – Thinking about and planning for what will happen when the project is finished. For example, trying to ensure that people are not left without any support in what they might do next and that everyone involved knows when it will end and how.

<u>Feedback</u> – Giving and receiving feedback is an important part of learning. Having done a project, programme or piece of work we need to know how we have done. Only then can we know how to improve. This is part of assessment, an aspect of learning that makes us apprehensive because it reveals weaknesses as well as strengths.

<u>Ground Rules</u> – Different aspects that need to be considered and agreed by the workers and the young adults in how they will work together. For example, what time any breaks might be and their duration, health and safety matters and other factors for example how to challenge certain behaviour and others in the group.

Mentor – The mentor is a generic term used to describe someone with whom young adults can develop a significant attachment. Acting as a guide, supporter and assessor, the mentor adds considerably to the value of the learning experience.

NSF – Neighbourhood Support Fund.

Secondary phase of education – Commonly referred to as 11- 16 key stages 1-5.

Self-awareness – Knowing and owning your own feelings, what you feel about things and recognising the range of feelings and what are the likely consequences of having them.

Social exclusion – Social exclusion is the term used to describe how some forms of disadvantage, including poverty, unemployment, poor skills and educational under-achievement interact to place some people on the margins of mainstream society. Social exclusion is about more than multiple disadvantages. It is about the effects that social inequalities and divisions, poverty, lack of power and lack of knowledge have on people's ability to participate, or to be taken seriously by others in society.

Social inclusion – Working through the constraints outlined above to ensure that people are included and have the opportunity to participate as they see fit without being in any way marginalised.

Soft skills – The easy way of defining soft skills is to think of what is needed for every day living in the 21st Century. These include working with others, problem solving and negotiation skills. Then also include personal qualities such as increased self-confidence and esteem, motivation, acknowledging and managing feelings and being self aware, with the determination and a willingness to learn.

Summary discussion – This usually refers to a discussion at the end of a process for example when a young person leaves a project. It provides an opportunity for giving and receiving feedback and reflection on what the young person and workers may have gained from the project.

Sustainability – The extent to which any work or activities started can survive and continue beyond the original or agreed funded period.

Synergy – The benefits accrued from working together.

Tertiary phase of education – Post 16 for example provided through Colleges of Further and Higher Education.

Further reading

National framework of informal education awards, 2002, National Youth Agency.

An insight into the Learning Gateway, 2002, Jackson, Carol, National Youth Agency/ National Institute for Adult Continuing Education. Available from: National Youth Agency, 17-23 Albion Street, Leicester LE1 6GD. (Tel: 0116 285 3700); www.nya.org.uk

Busted: an interactive approach to decision making and citizenship, 2002, Information Plus.

People skills for young adults, 2000, Csoti, Marianna & Jessica Kingsley. Available from: Information Plus, 3 Hill of Heddle, Finstown, Orkney KW17 2LH. (Tel: 01856 761 334); www.information-plus.co.uk

Personality, 2001, Hopson, Barrie, Trotman. www.careers-portal.co.uk

Developing social skills: a learning resource manual for trainers and educators working in non-traditional learning environments (BTN) [accession code: 19861], 1999, Squirrell, Gillian, Russell House Publishing. Available from: Russell House Publishing, 4 St. George's House, The Business Park, Uplyme Road, Lyme Regis, Dorset, DT7 3LS. (Tel: 01297 443 948).

The youth service multi media handbook: a practical handbook for integrating multi media with youth work (QP:XDK) [accession code: 22303], 1999, Chalmers, Joseph, ed., Irish Youth Work Press. Available from: National Youth Federation, 20 Lower Dominick Street, Dublin 1. (Tel: 01 8729933).

Useful contacts and networks

The Wild Project, Jo Davies, 61 Lemon Street, Truro TR1 2PE.
Tel: 01872 260655. Fax: 01872 260099.

Connect 2, David Finn, Derbyshire County Youth Service, Middleton House, 27 St Mary's Gate, Derby DE1 3NN.
Tel: 01332 716956. Fax: 01332 716920. E-mail: david.finn@Derby.gov.uk

For more information about REMIT please telephone 0116 2995791.

Steps Forward Mentoring Programme, Becki Rowe, Newcastle YMCA, 180 Portland Road, Newcastle Upon Tyne NE2 1DJ. Tel: 0191 230 4710. Fax: 0191 221 1779.

All Change, Gurpreet Sidhu, 16-34 Graham Street , London N1 8JX.
Tel: 020 7689 4646. Fax: 020 689 4647. E-mail: all.change@virgin.net

Step Project, Liza Darroch, Impact Youth Centre, Lewis Lane, Cirencester GL7 1XA.
Tel: 01285 640994. Fax: 01285 644171. E-mail: eqd@cirencester.ac.uk

Route 43, Rosie Croarkin, Woodhouse Park Youth Centre, Portway, Wythenshaw, Manchester M22 6QW.
Tel: 0161 498 8755. Fax: 0161 437 7642. E-mail: route43@zoom.co.uk

Care 2 Share, Karen Hammett, Young People's Centre, 69 Ship Street, Brighton BN1 1AE.
Tel: 01273 230130. Fax: 01273 722168. E-mail: ypc@pact.org.uk

Aylestone Lifeskills, YMCA Leicester, 7 East Street, Leicester LE1 6EY.

Befrienders Project, 102 North Street, Barking IG11 8LA.